Book of Borders, Rules, Corners & Ornaments

Book of Borders, Rules, Corners & Ornaments

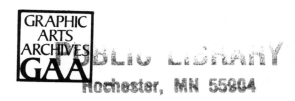

Sterling Publishing Co., Inc.   New York

Library of Congress Cataloging-in-Publication Data

McCord, Robert R.
 Book of borders, rules, corners & ornaments / Robert R. McCord.
   p.   cm.
  ISBN 0-8069-8236-5
  1. Type ornaments.   2. Printers' ornaments.   3. Borders,
Ornamental (Decorative arts)   4. Printing—History—19th century—
Specimens.   I. Title.
Z250.3.M33   1991   90-27460
686.2′24—dc20   CIP

Designed by Bob Feldgus

10   9   8   7   6   5   4   3   2   1

A Robert R. McCord Book

Published in 1991 by Sterling Publishing Company, Inc.,
387 Park Avenue South, New York, N.Y. 10016.
© 1991 by Robert R. McCord Inc.
Distributed in Canada by Sterling Publishing,
% Canadian Manda Group, P.O. Box 920, Station U,
Toronto, Ontario, Canada M8Z 5P9.
Distributed in Great Britain and Europe by Cassell PLC,
Villiers House, 41/47 Strand, London WC2N 5JE, England.
Distributed in Australia by Capricorn Ltd.,
P.O. Box 665, Lane Cove, NSW 2066.
Manufactured in the United States of America
All rights reserved

Sterling ISBN 0-8069-8236-5

Contents

INTRODUCTION

The Book of Borders, Rules, Corners & Ornaments is a unique collection of copyright-free design elements which will be of use to the artist and graphic designer. It may be used equally well by people who put together their own invitations or greeting cards, sale flyers or announcements, stationery or notepads. These engraved images reproduce with great clarity and faithfulness and may be enlarged or reduced with no loss in quality. They provide the finishing touch to any typographic design. Derived from original sources including 19th-century type books, these designs may be used as is or adopted to make derivative but unique images.

Robert Feldgus, an accomplished designer, has assisted in the selection of the design elements in this book. He has helped to choose those borders, rules, corners and ornaments that will be of greatest use and versatility to the individual designer. Each of the design elements will help to set a mood and create an impression when used with type. Ranging from the simple to the ornate, there is a design element in this book which can enhance any project.

The addition of a border or a rule, a corner or an ornament, can change the whole feel of a printed piece. Given that all of the elements in **The Book of Borders, Rules, Corners & Ornaments** are in the public domain, you can creatively use or adapt them for your own artistic purposes.

BORDERS

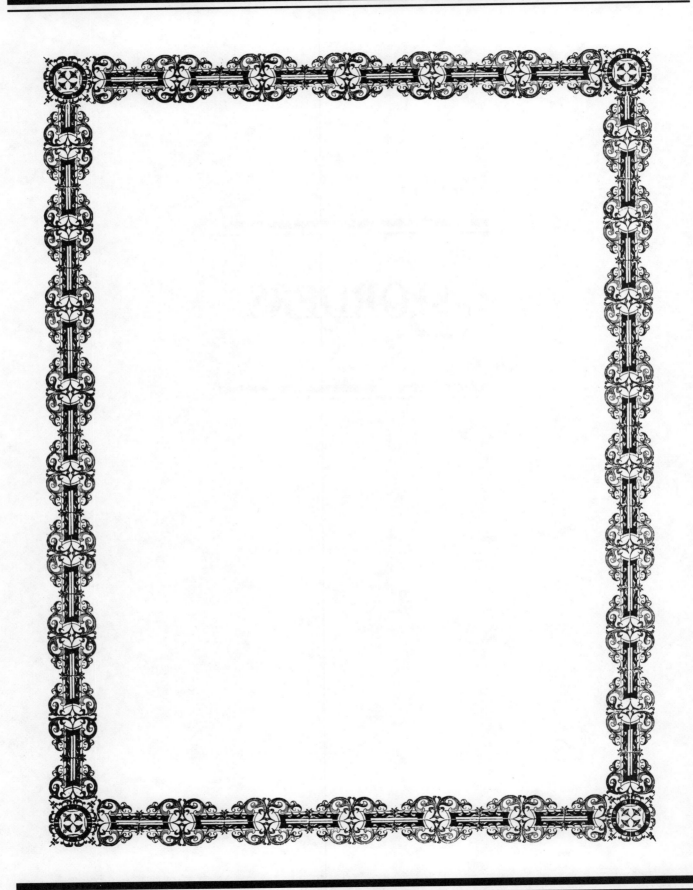

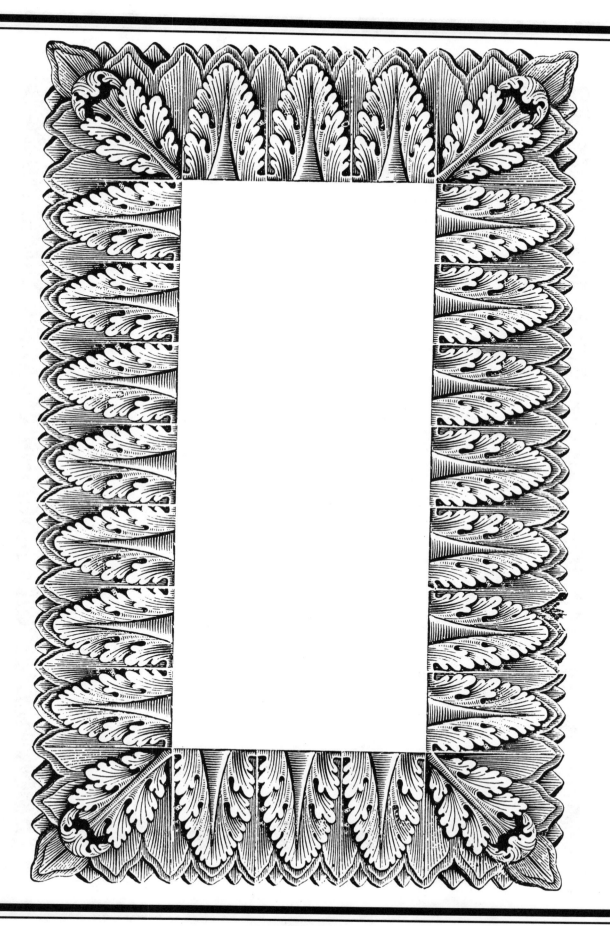

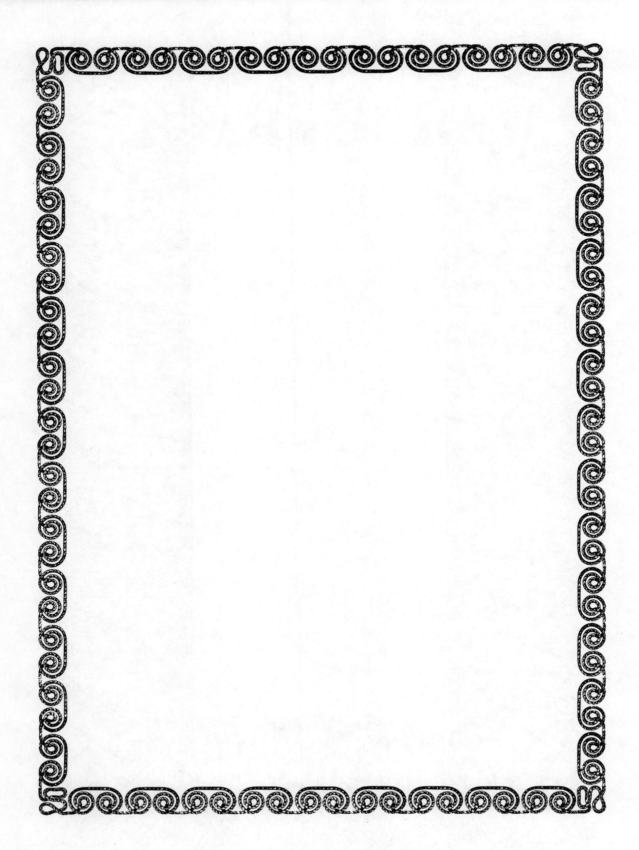

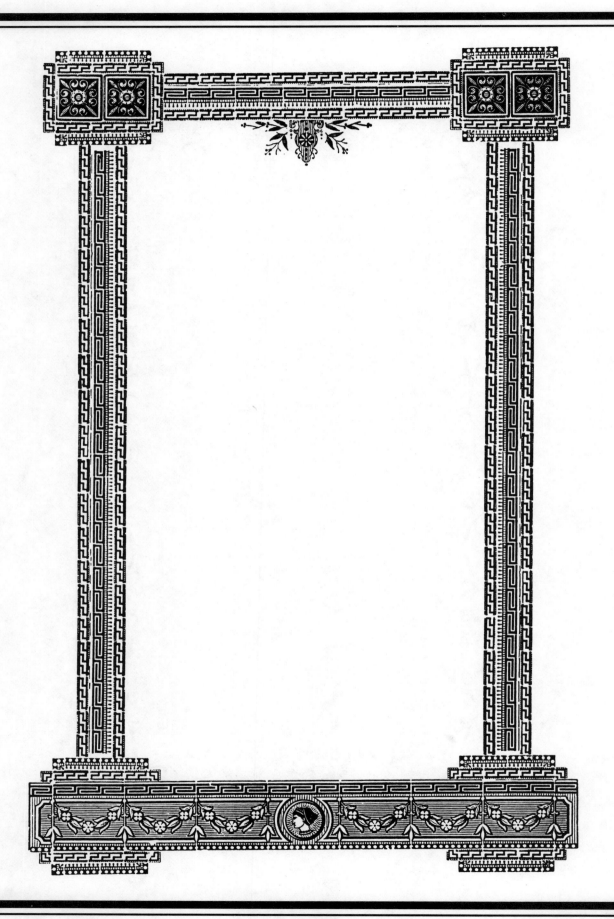

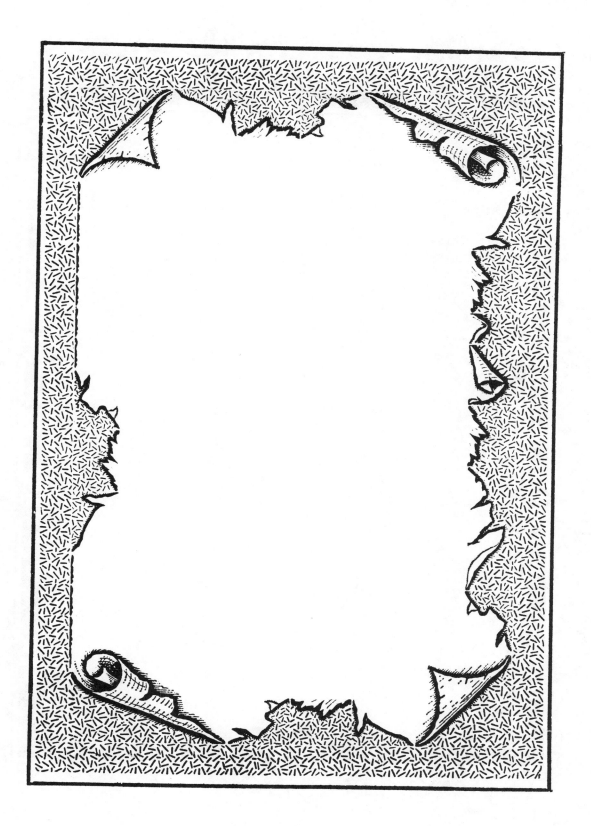

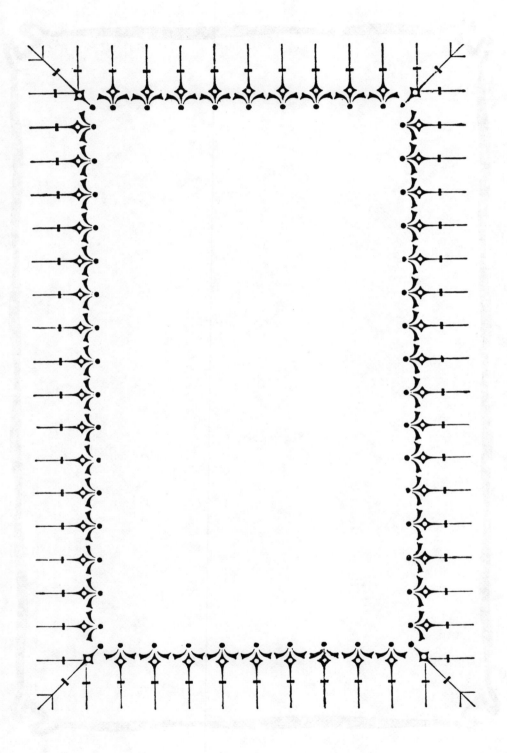

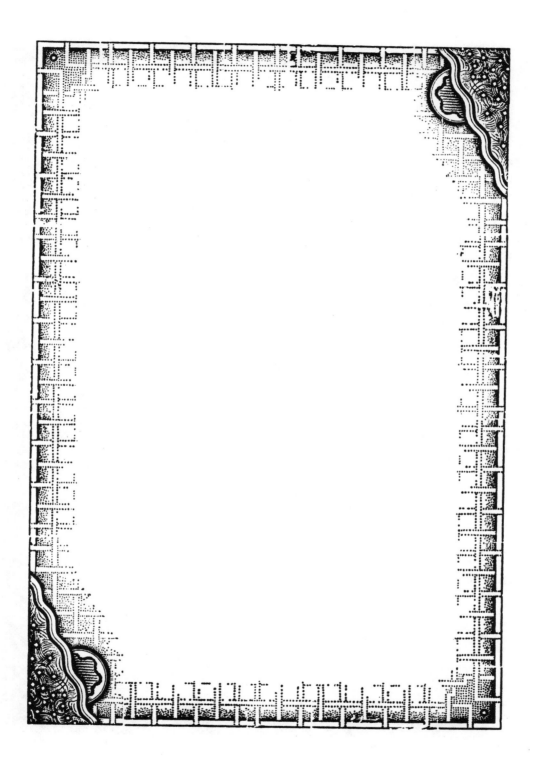

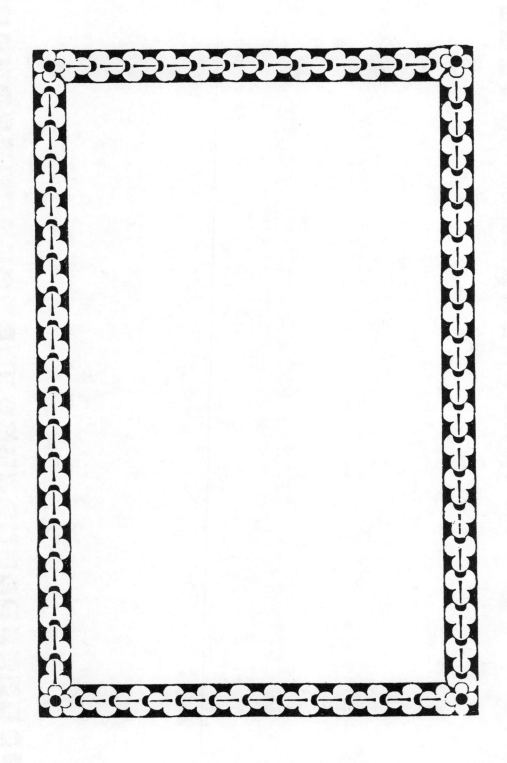

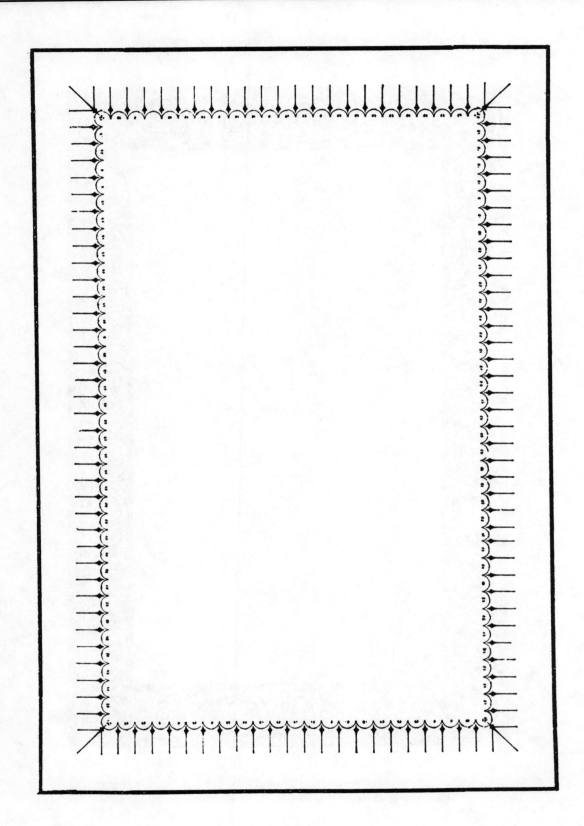

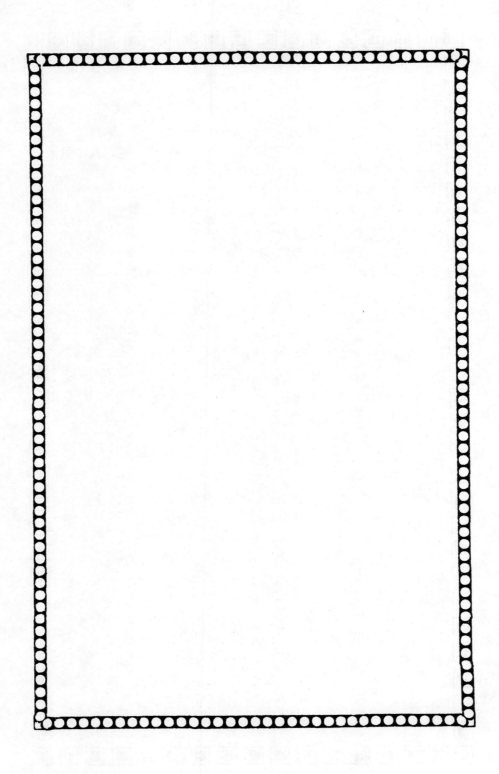

RULES

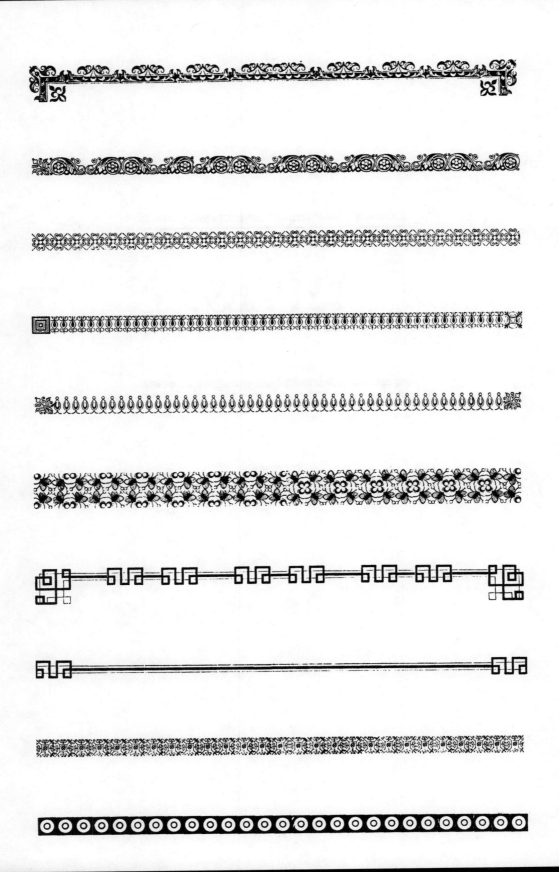

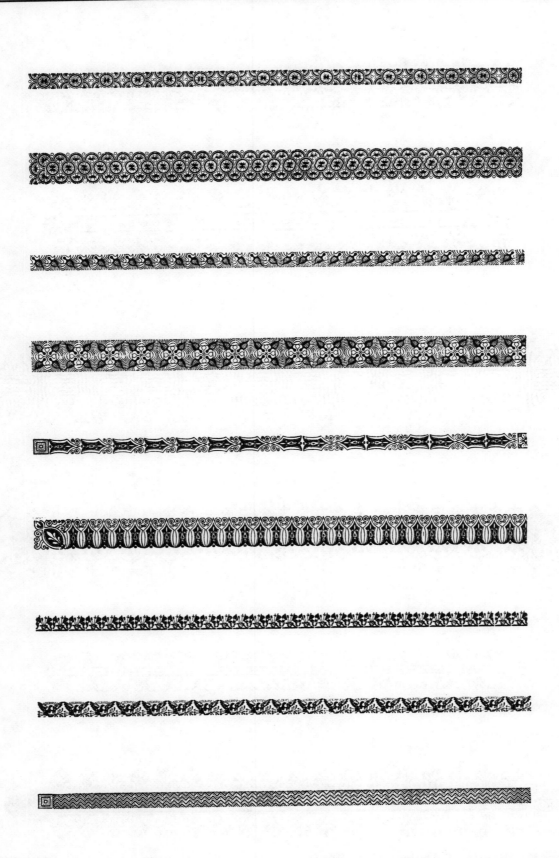

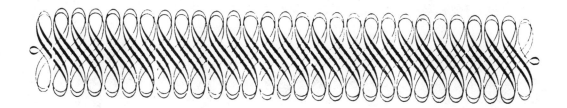

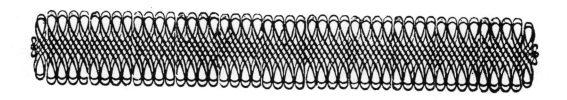

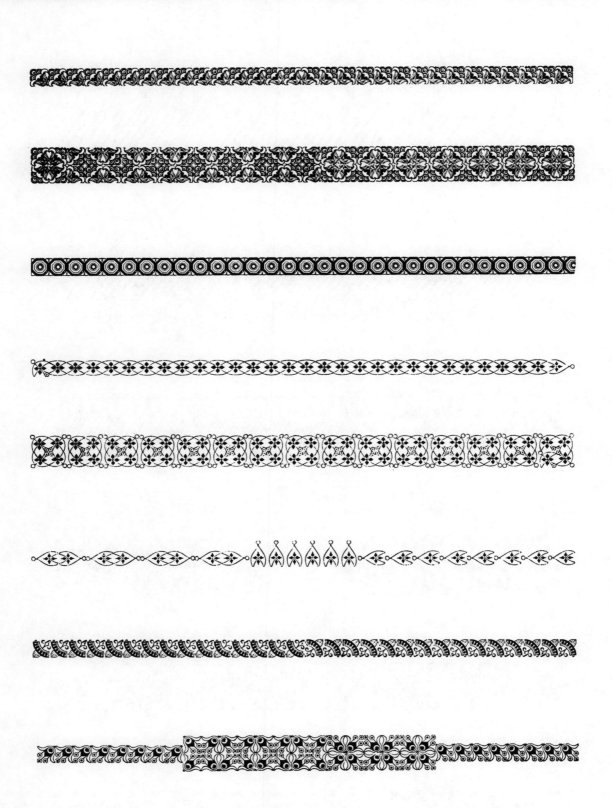

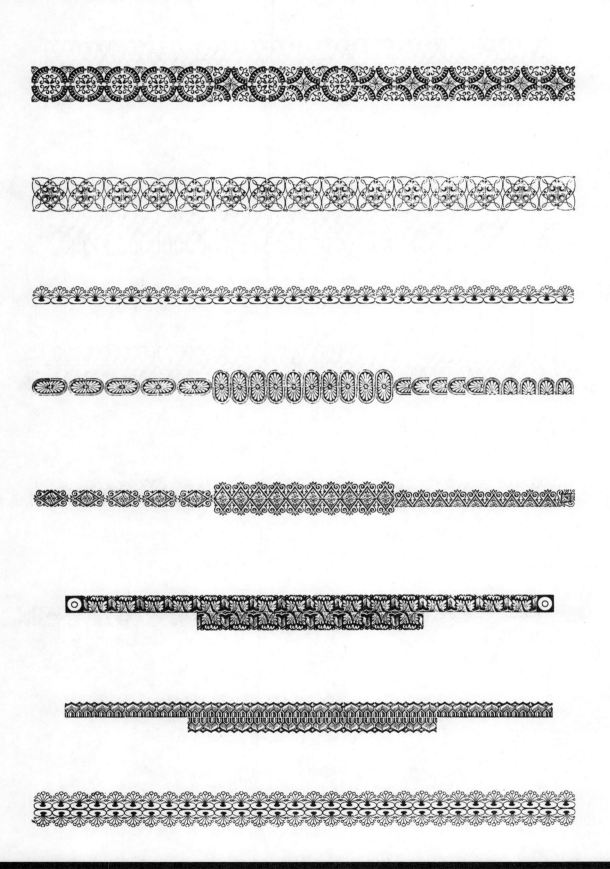

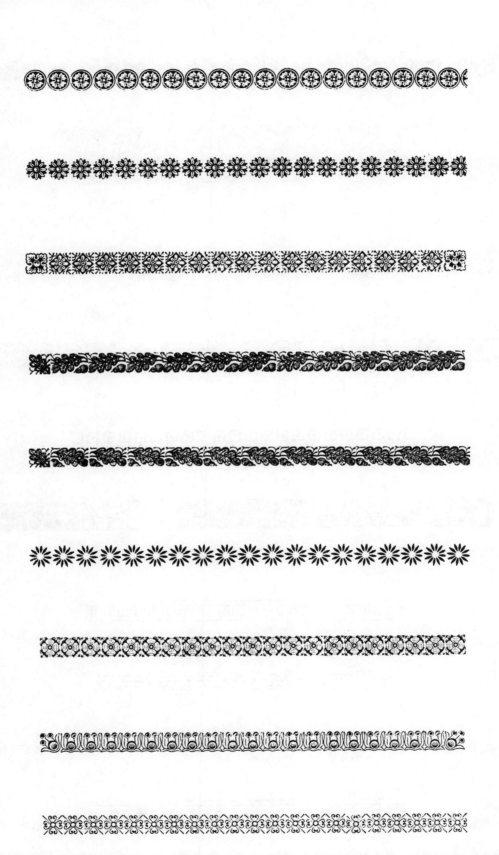

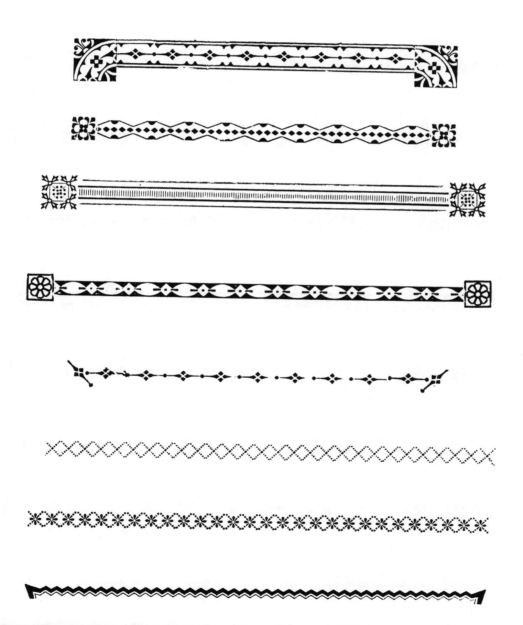

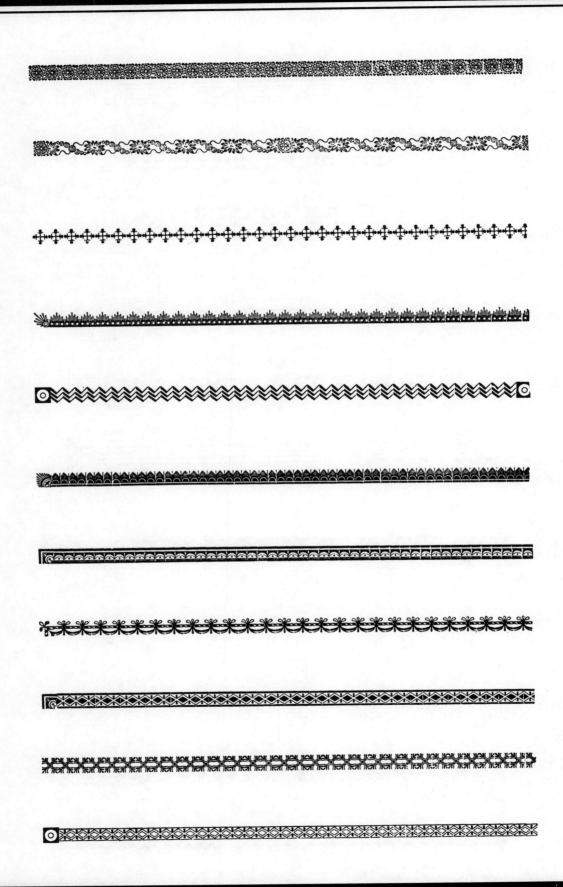

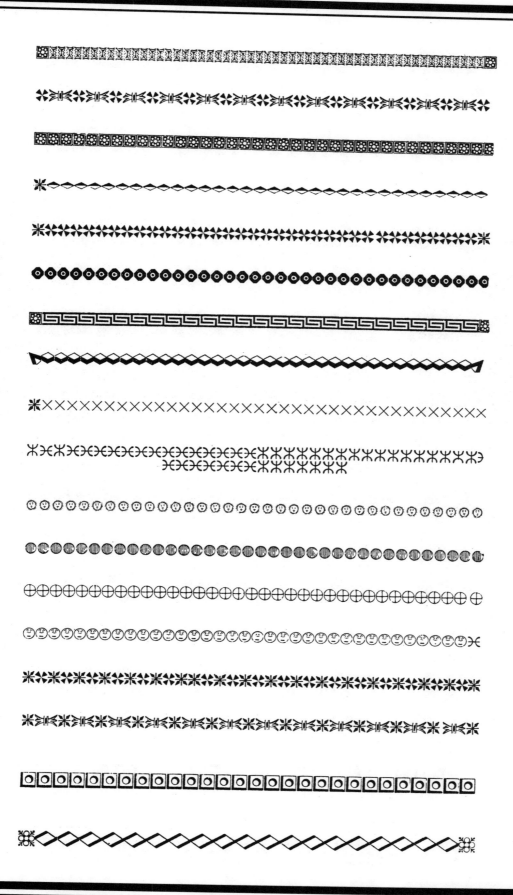

CORNERS
&
ORNAMENTS

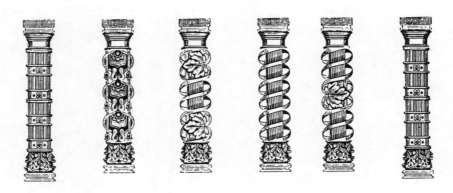

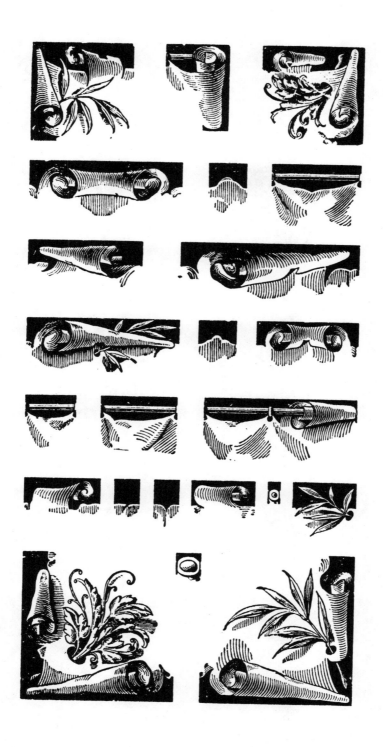

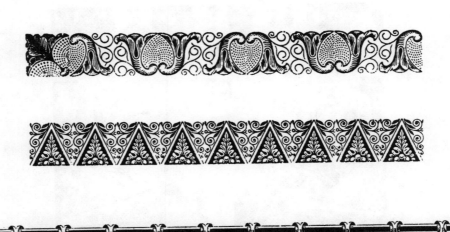

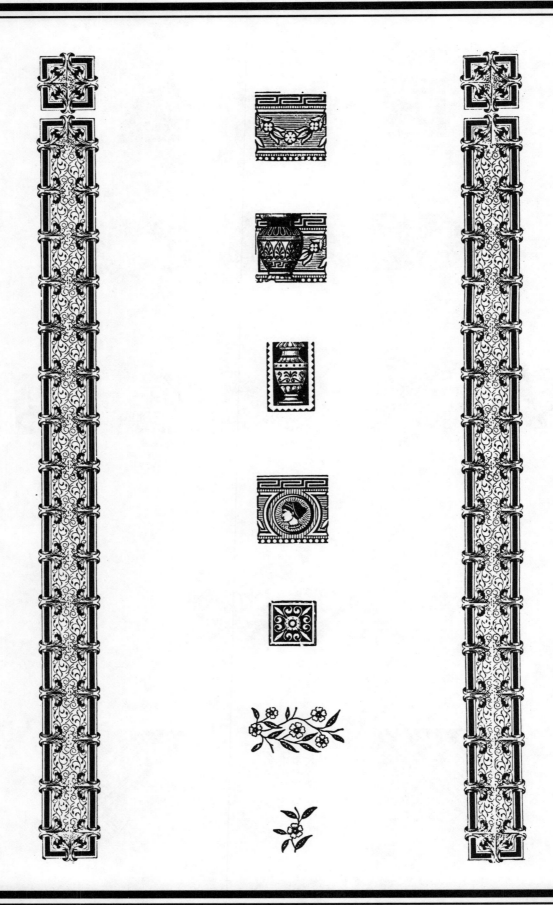

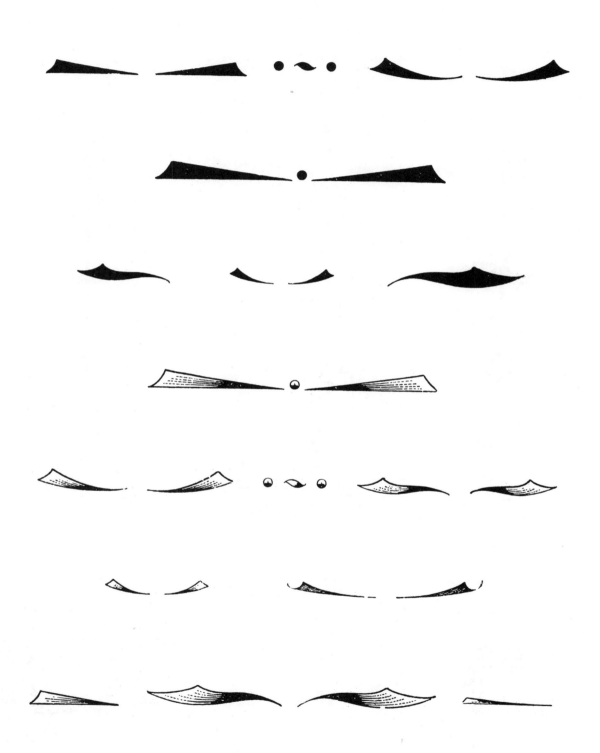

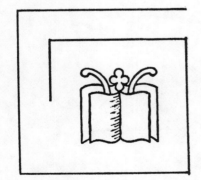

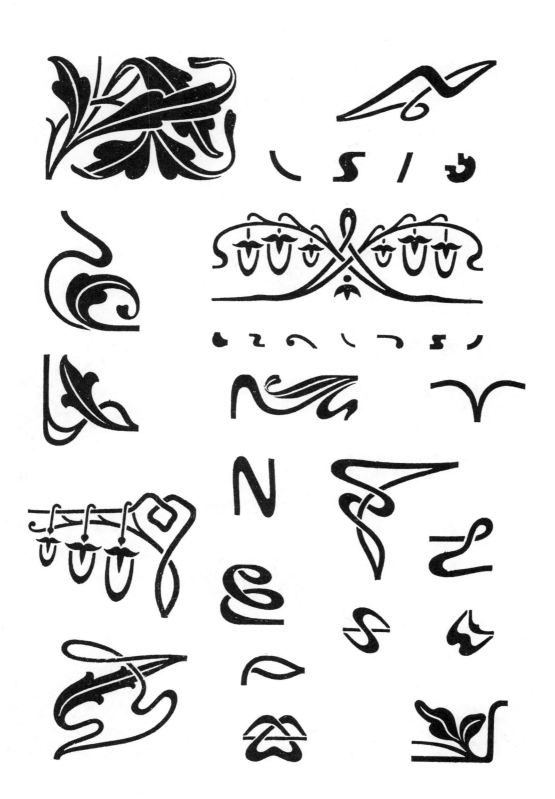

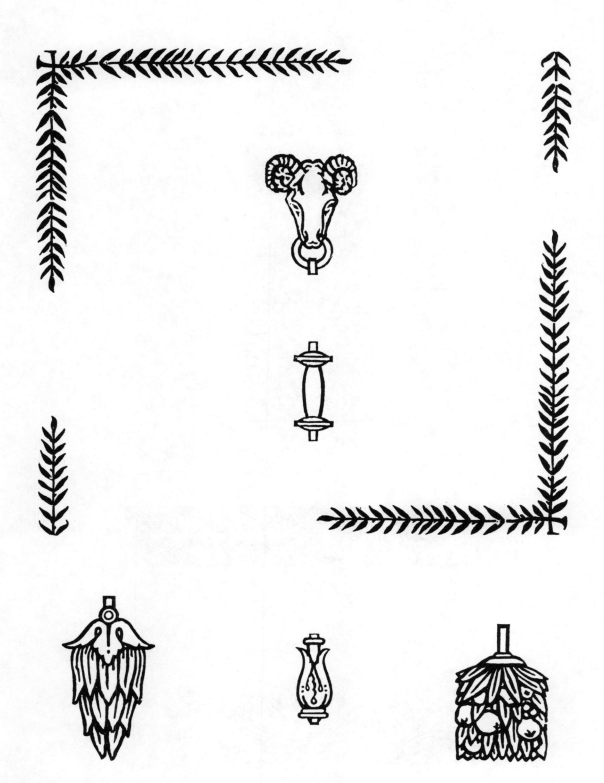

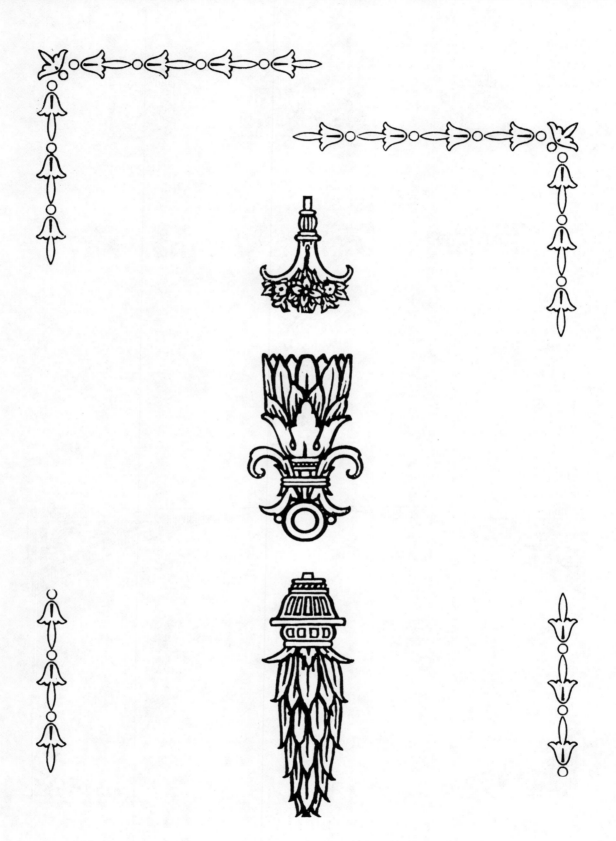

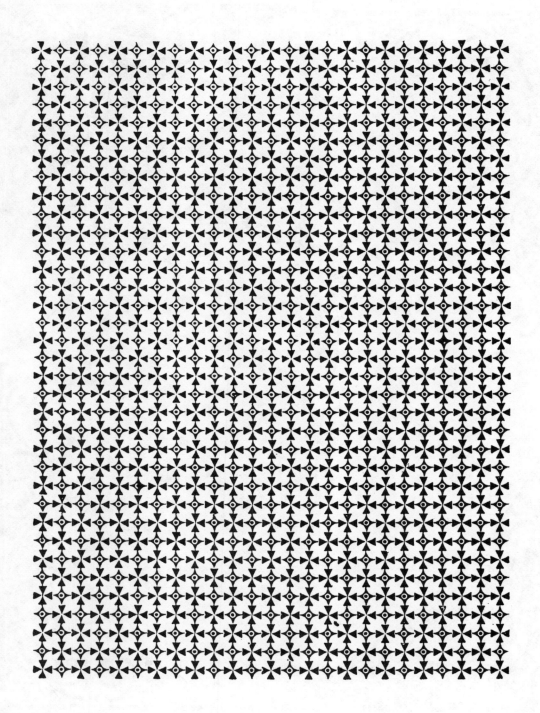

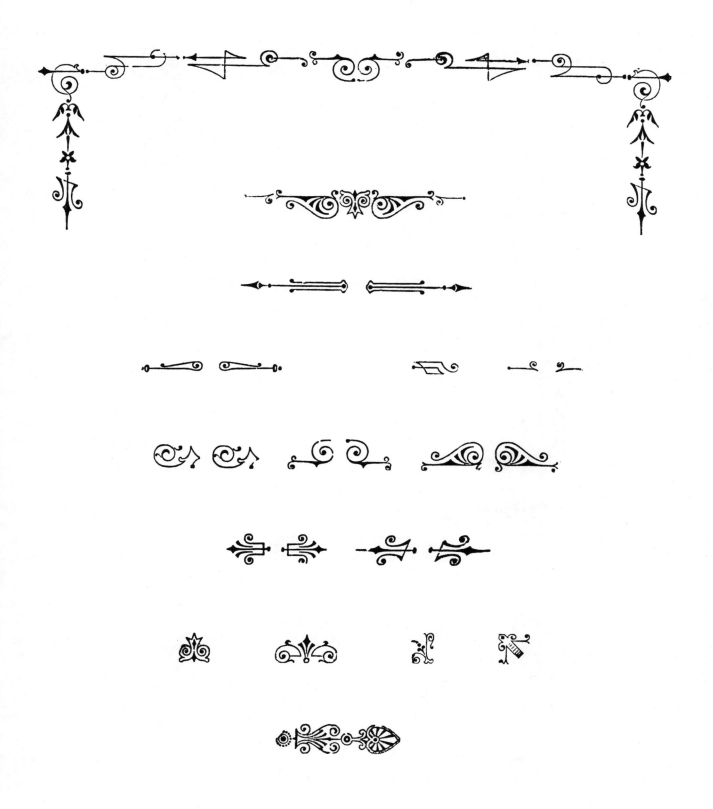

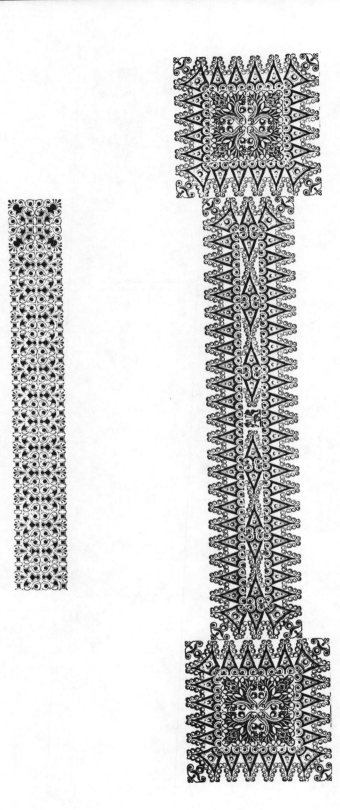

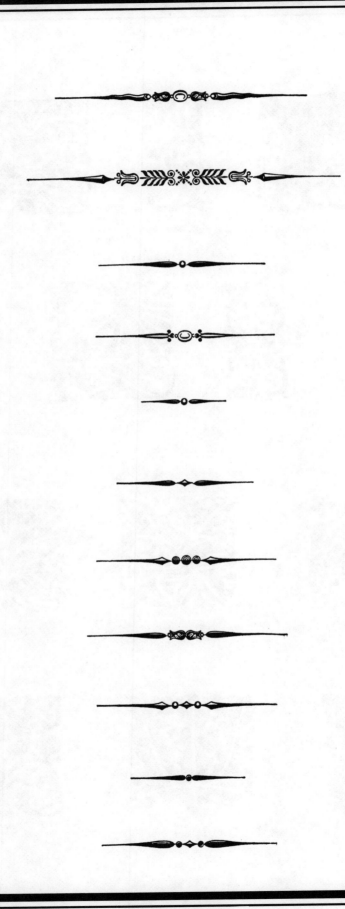

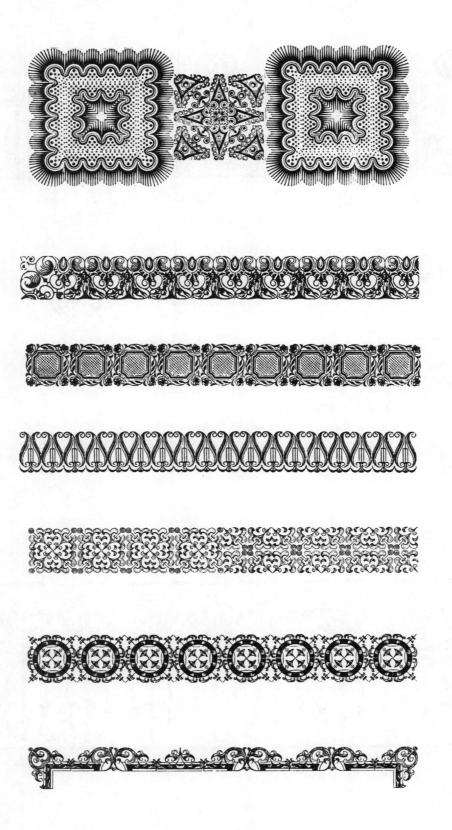

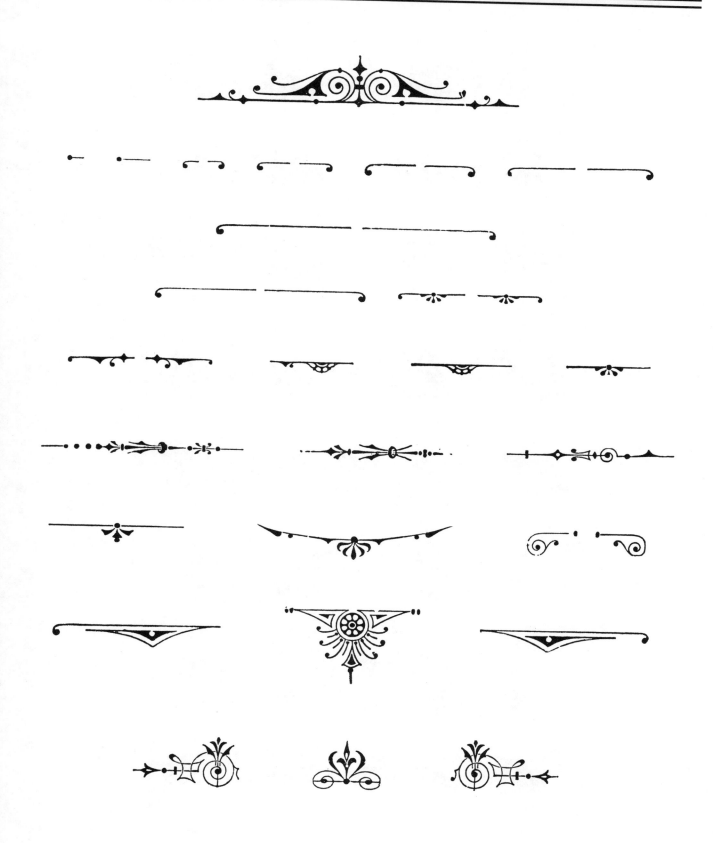

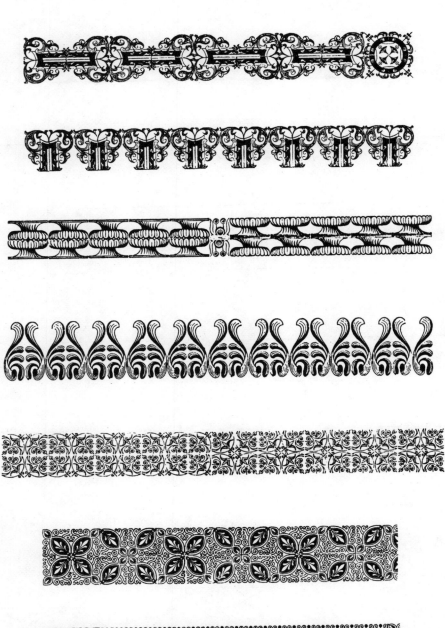

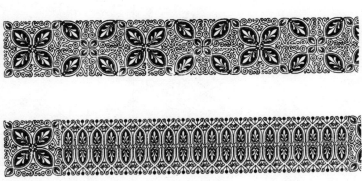

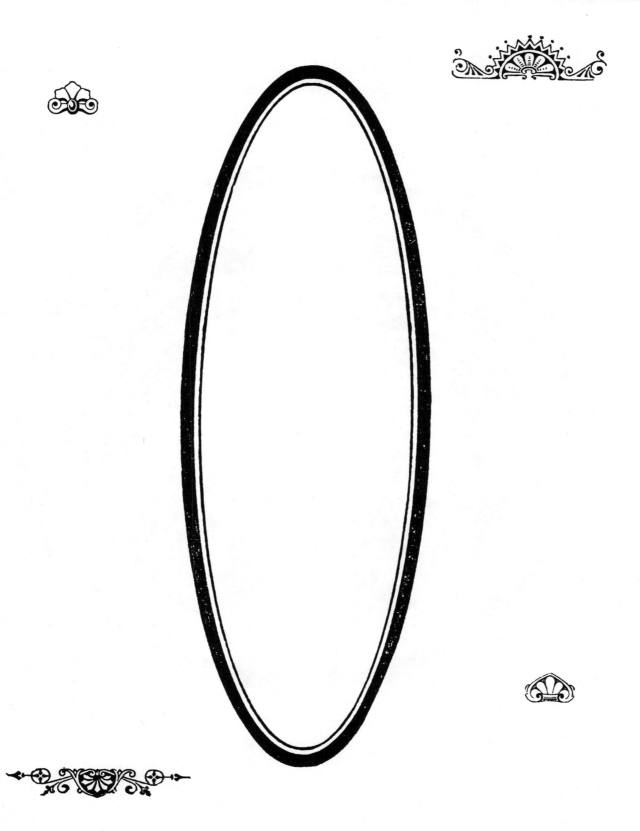

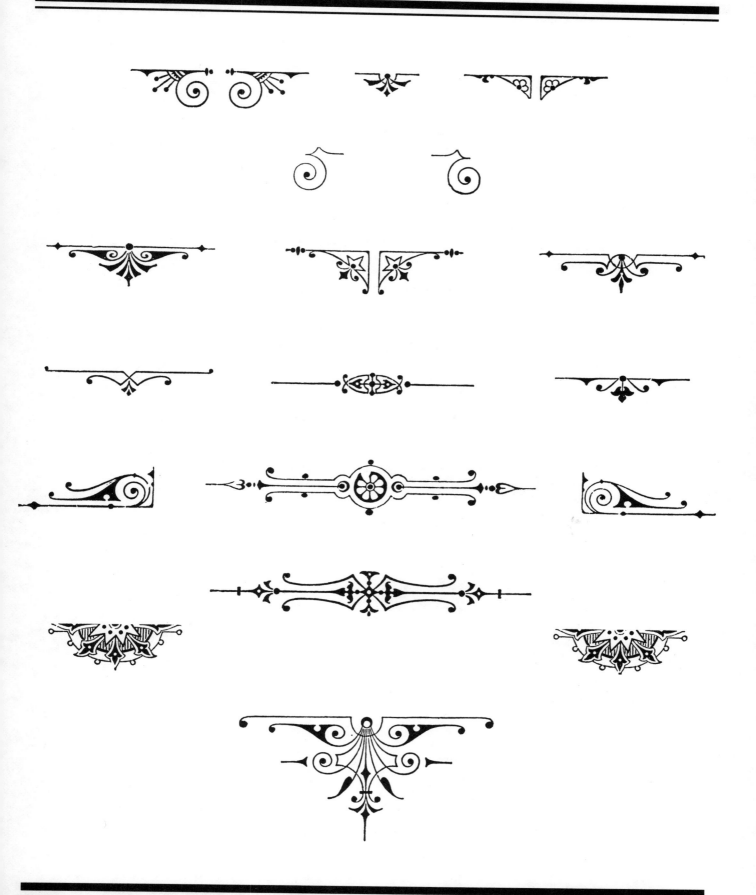

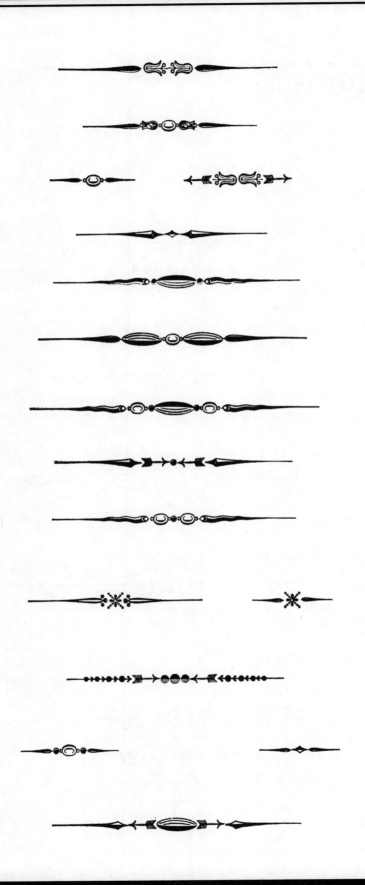

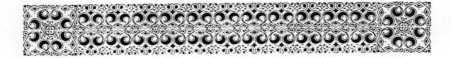

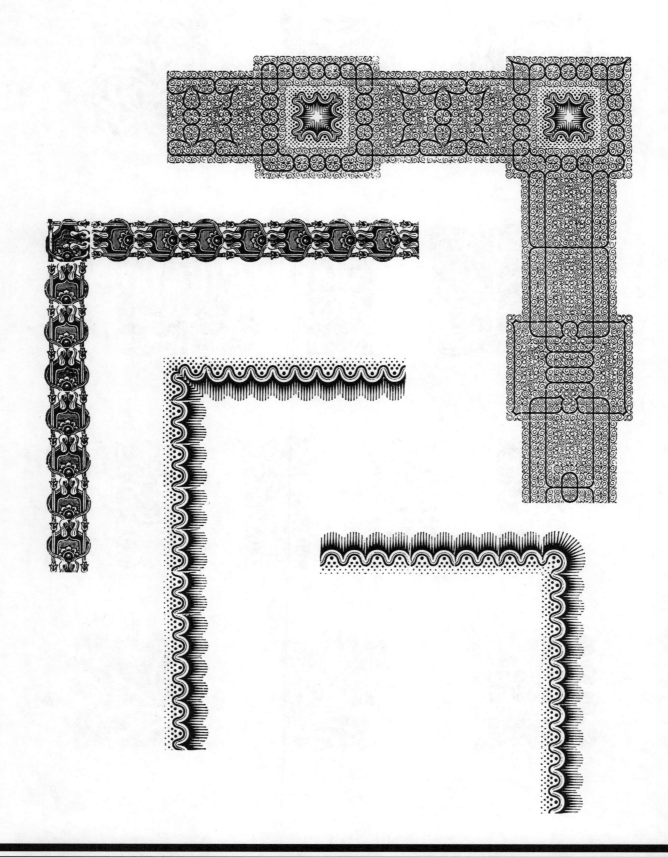

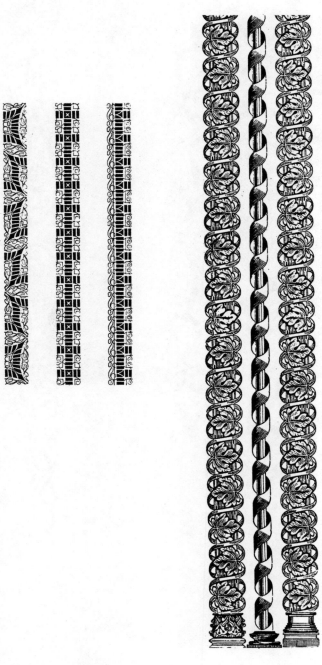

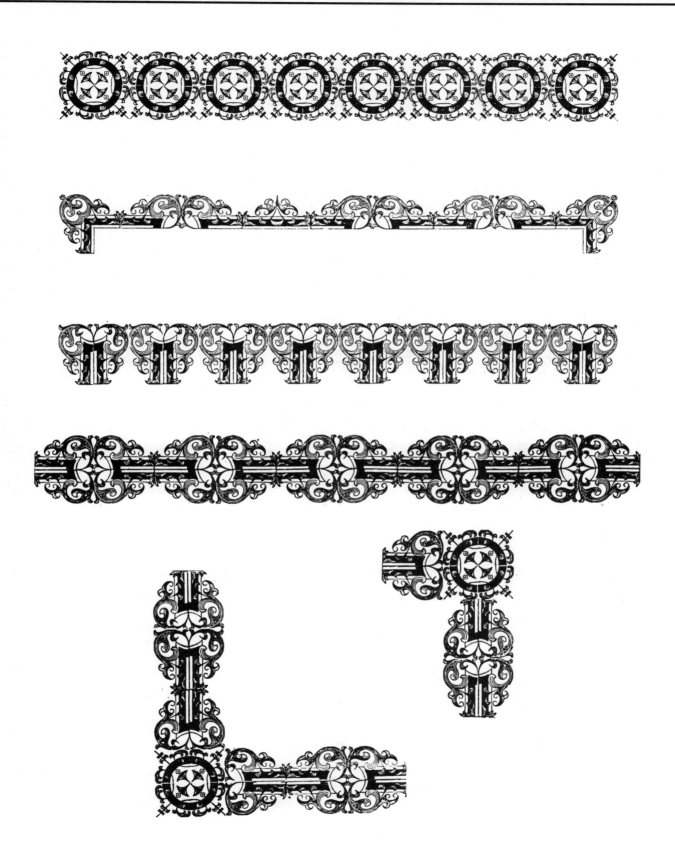

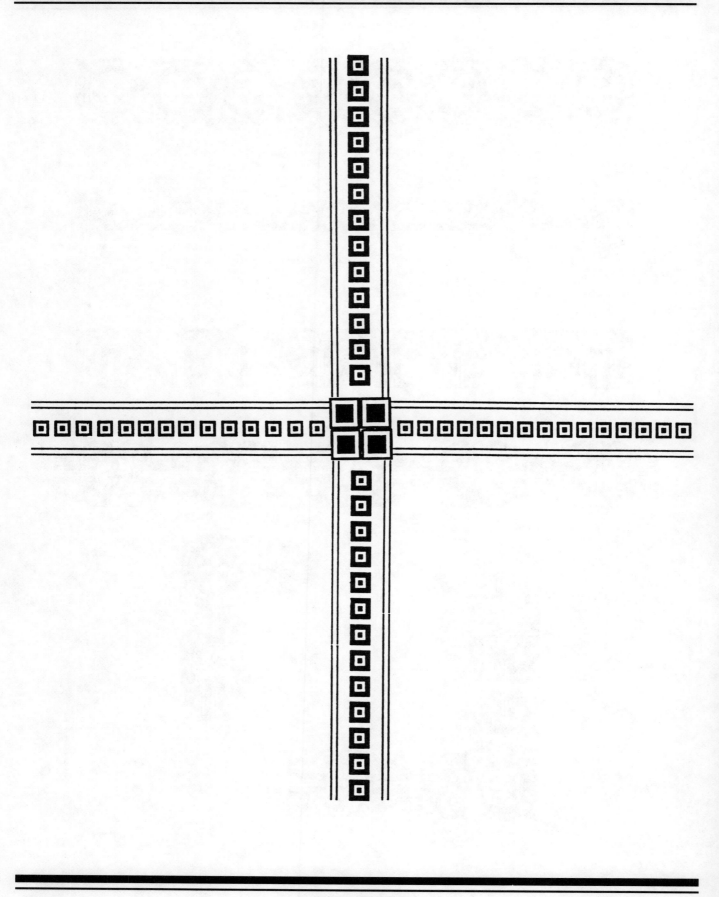

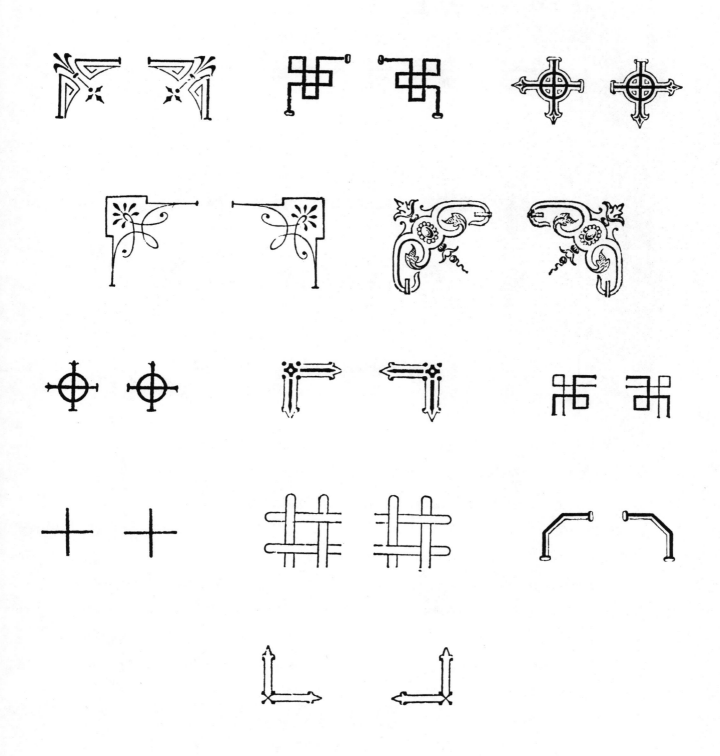

115

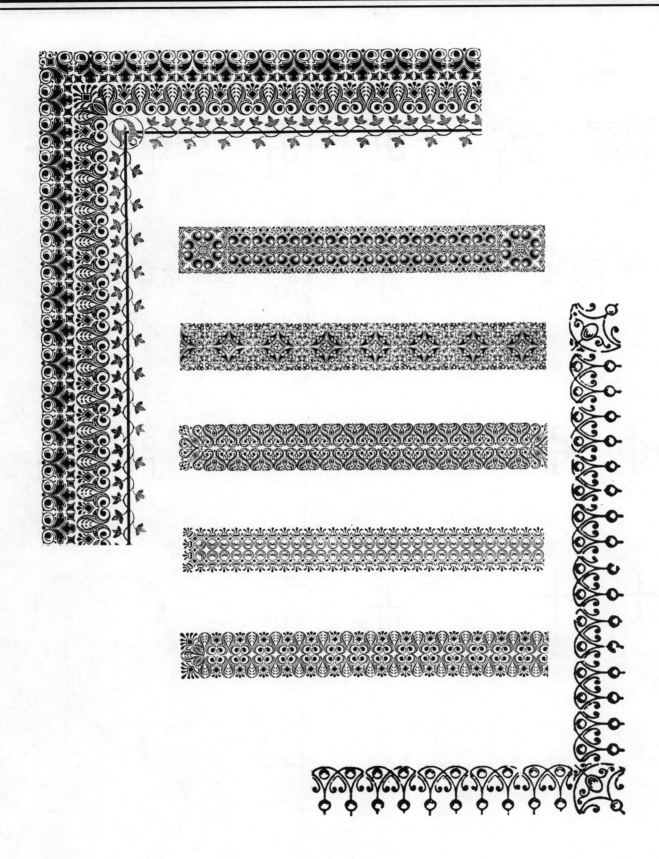

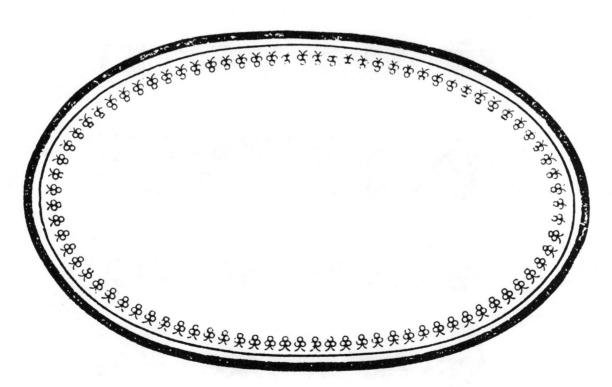

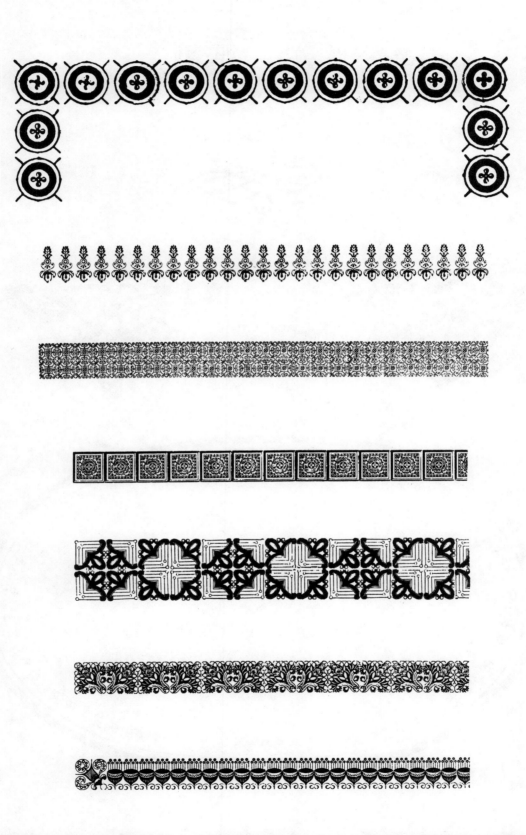

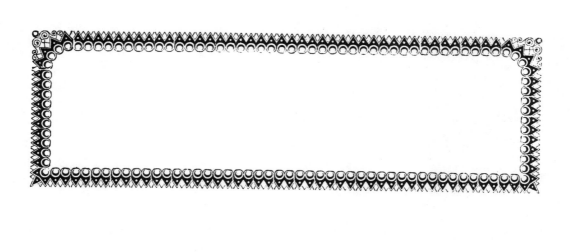

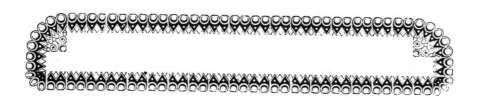

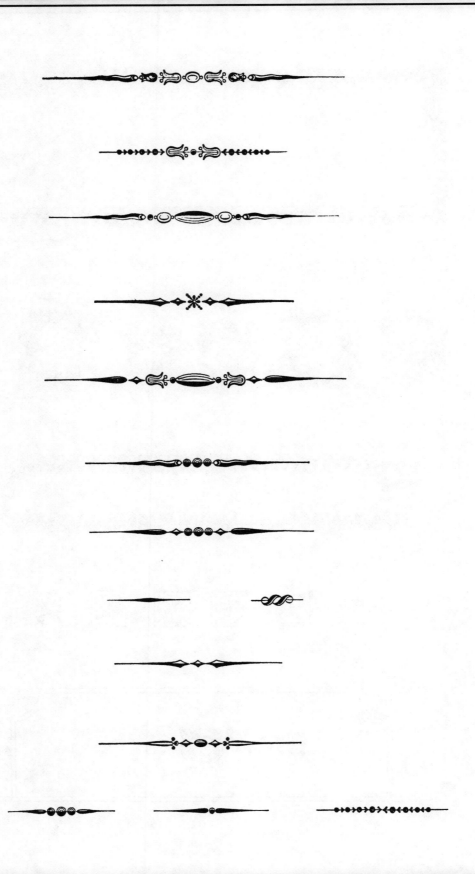

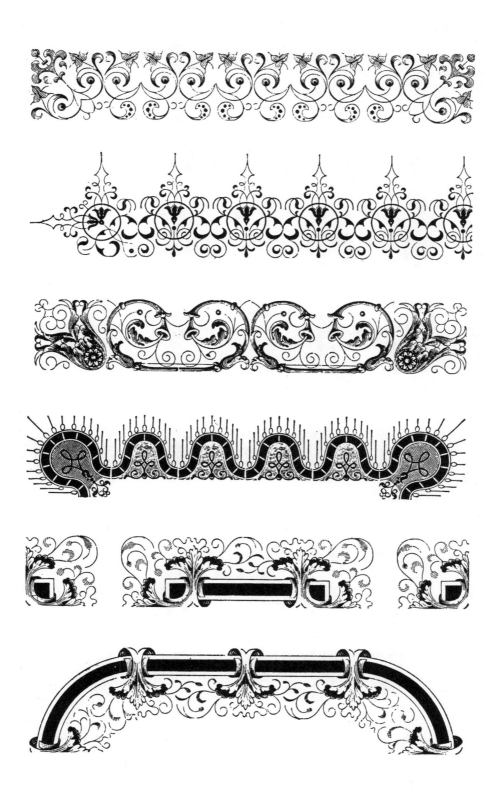

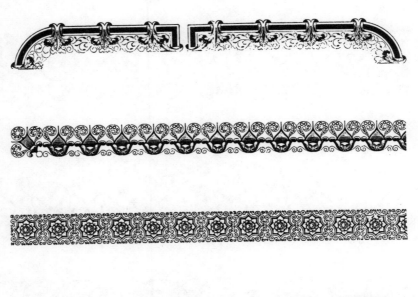

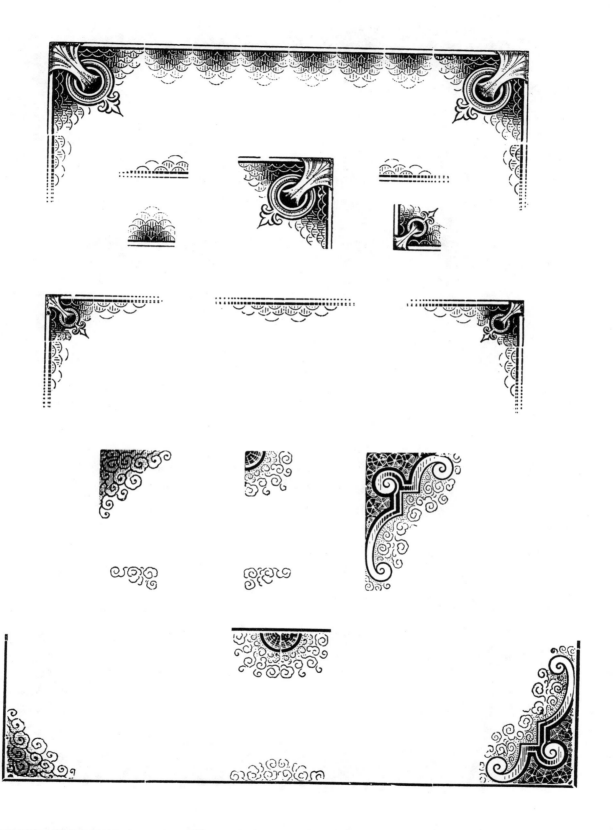

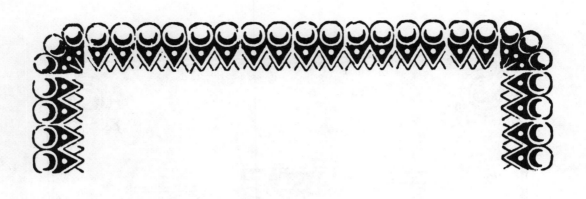

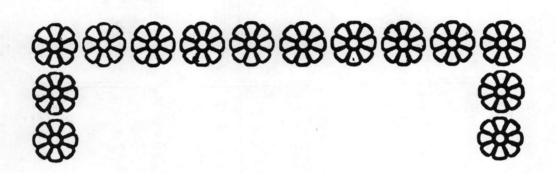

126

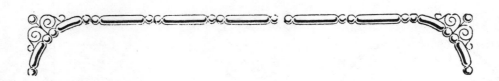

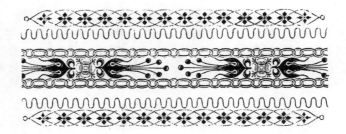